Indians

Indians
Robin May

Exeter Books
NEW YORK

🐃 A Bison Book

For

ALLAN

and

MARION RADBOURNE

PAGE 1: *A Hidatsa warrior in the costume of the Dog Dance.*

TITLE PAGE: *Horse travois of the Plains Indians.*

THIS PAGE: *The Snowshoe Dance of the Chippewa.*

CONTENTS

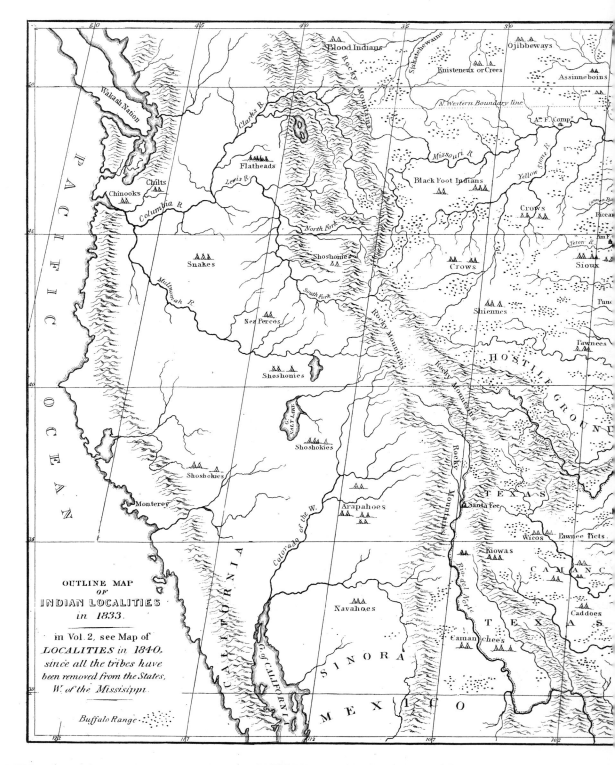

OUTLINE MAP
OF
INDIAN LOCALITIES
in 1833.

in Vol. 2, see Map of
LOCALITIES in 1840.
since all the tribes have
been removed from the States,
W. of the Mississipi

Buffalo Range

INTRODUCTION AND ACKNOWLEDGMENTS

This book concentrates almost entirely on the Native Americans of what is now the United States. Space permits only a handful of tribes to be described in any detail, otherwise any narrative flow would be impossible. Other tribes are featured at key moments in their history, while many more can be tracked down elsewhere by the interested reader—tribes such as the Winnebago, the Assiniboin, the Kickapoo and dozens more which held the stage for moments of brief fame and less brief tragedy.

Most of this book is about the trans-Mississippi West from the 1850s to 1890, the year of Wounded Knee, though there is a chapter about the Indians of the East who had faced much earlier, in the Colonial period, most of the same

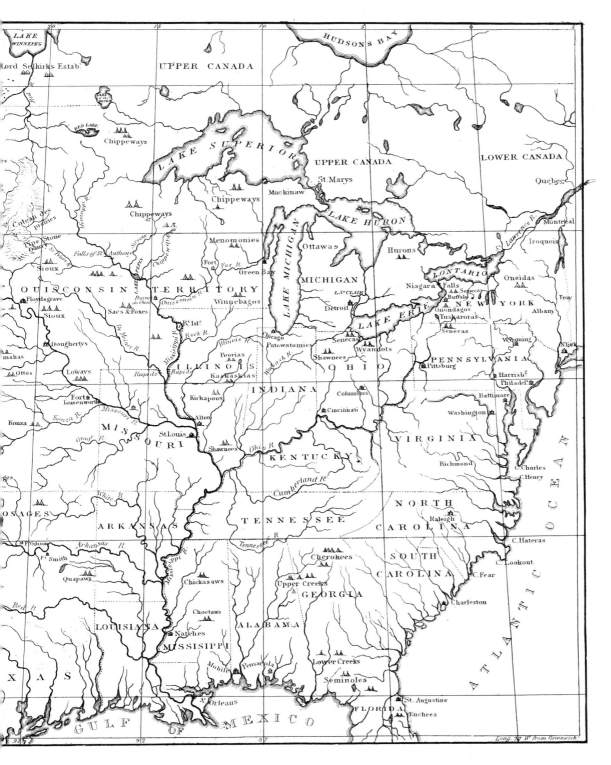

problems with the whites as did the tribes in the West.

The spelling of Indian names and words follows Webster's *Third New International Dictionary*.

The state historical societies of Arizona, South Dakota, Montana, Wyoming and Kansas are among the organizations to which I am grateful. It is in highly researched articles in their journals that previously accepted facts are so often revealed to be untrue. I am particularly grateful to Allan Radbourne for helping me with the complexities of the Apache Wars, and to Robert A Utley, whose books are exactly what scholarly histories of the Indian Wars ought to be but so rarely are. I also owe a great debt to my wife, Maureen, for her encouragement and help.

Robin May

Many Indian tribes worshipped natural phenomena, as seen in Invocation to the Sun, *by Charles M. Russell.*

1
NATIVE AMERICANS

It happened just before the final tragedy at Wounded Knee brought the Indian Wars to an end. The date was September 1890; the place, Lame Deer in Montana; the Indians involved, two Northern Cheyennes called Head Chief and John Young Mule. Twenty-five-year-old Head Chief was a troublemaker, partly because he was bitter that he had never had a chance to prove himself as a warrior. He was fond of the daughter of Chief American Horse. Food was short, and when the girl told Head Chief this, he went hunting with an orphan boy, John Young Mule, who was 13 or 14 years old.

They set out after deer, but instead shot a cow that belonged to a settler named Gaffney. They had just finished butchering it when Gaffney's nephew, Hugh Boyle, rode up. Young Mule, who had been to school and understood English, told Head Chief that Boyle had said: 'He called us dogs.'

Head Chief grabbed his rifle, shot Boyle and buried him in a shallow grave. Young Mule later reported that Boyle had actually said: 'I see a hungry dog has snapped up one of our cows.'

Soldiers were soon looking for the missing Boyle, first finding his horse, then bloodstains.

BELOW: Conquistadores setting war dogs on some Indians.

RIGHT: An engraving made in 1590, The Arrival of the Englishmen in Virginia, *by Theodor de Bry.*

FAR RIGHT ABOVE: Another de Bry engraving of 16th century Virginia Indians. BELOW: Virginia Indians Cooking Fish *by John White (1590).*

Pasquenoke.

MEO

Trinety harbor

T.B

TOP: *A painting of about 1500 showing the various costumes of the Aztec Indians in Mexico.*

ABOVE: *Another painting of the same period showing the war costumes and weapons of the Aztecs.*

RIGHT: *This 16th century painting shows a battle between the Aztec Indians and Cortez's troops.*

A view of the Interior of the Lodge of a Mandan Chief, *painted about 1839 by the artist Karl Bodmer.*

Meanwhile, the Cheyenne were expecting the whites to attack their camp. When Head Chief realized this, he told American Horse what had happened and. asked him to let the soldiers know that he was the guilty one. He would not be hanged, but would fight them all in the open.

Young Mule came to Head Chief and said that he would die with him. 'When you are dead, I will have nothing,' he explained. They spent that last night talking on a hill.

At sunrise, the time had come to die. Below the hill were hundreds of Cheyenne, and also cavalry and infantry facing the braves, ready, if necessary, to put down an uprising.

The two Indians charged down the hill, then wheeled up again. Young Mule's horse was hit on the way up and had to be led to the top; then the young man started down the hill again on foot, shooting, zigzagging, taking cover, and shooting again until he was killed. Head Chief, who had told his friends that he would ride straight through the soldiers, donned his grandfather's war bonnet and charged down the hill at a gallop. Hit time and again by bullets, he

was still charging through the dismounted soldiers when an officer shot him fatally. The soldiers went away, leaving the Cheyenne to tend to their dead.

That small-scale fight combines the fact and the myth of the American Indian. It is a classic reminder that the story of the American West was not romantic but epic. For many, mounted Plains Indians like the Cheyenne typify the Native Americans, yet most of the northern Plains Indians were mounted for little more than a century—a small part of the 30,000 or so years in which there had been Indians in the Americas.

'Indians' is as vague a word as 'Europeans'. Columbus coined the name when he thought he had reached the Indies—India—in 1492. In recent times 'Amerind' has been coined, though the more recent 'Native American' is a happier phrase. For the purpose of this book, however,

14

Indian will be used. As for calling them 'Red-men', some of the first white men to land in the East saw quite light-skinned Indians. When they tanned in the summer, their skins became reddish, then a fine copper color.

Down the centuries, white attitudes toward Indians have tended to follow two courses, the 'painted savage' or the 'noble savage/down-trodden native'. The vast majority of frontier whites believed bitterly in the first portrait, while farther East, which had once been a frontier, there was more sympathy with the unfortunate Indians. Since the 1950s, the shame of present-day Americans has been based more on an awakened conscience than on knowledge of what the West was really like. It has so distorted the picture that many well-meaning readers of propaganda rather than history have turned the American Indian into an idealized being persecuted by wicked whites, as if all Indians were like the noble Chief Joseph of the Nez Percé and all whites like the monstrous Colonel Chivington of Sand Creek. The truth, of course, lies in between. Indians and whites were—people. Which is not to say that the stricken conscience of many white people is not justified. The Native Americans were greatly wronged and many still are.

Today's revised version of the Indians is as simplistic as the 'painted savage' school of thought. The Indians are praised as ecologists, as warriors who preferred peace, as natural democrats, as a superb example of communal people and as people who understood the natural world. Only the first and the last stand up as generalizations. As Frederick William Turner III has put it, having characterized the harshness of Indian life, 'he never lost sight of the fact that all this was distinctively, essentially, radically human, that he was human and thus part of the universal community of the living.' The harshness included the fact that old people

OPPOSITE TOP LEFT: An Osage Indian holding a pipe-tomahawk.
OPPOSITE TOP RIGHT: Bird Rattler, a Blackfoot Indian; photograph taken in 1916 in Browning, Montana.
OPPOSITE CENTER: A Nootka whaling Indian from the Northwest Coast.
OPPOSITE BOTTOM LEFT: A Southern Cheyenne, Wolf Robe (Ho Nihewoomah), 1909.
OPPOSITE BOTTOM RIGHT: White Swan, a Crow warrior, with his stone club and rawhide shield.

were often brutally treated and that women were usually regarded as second-class citizens.

Before noting what many tribes had in common, let us note a few of the extreme contrasts. Some were caused by geography, others were not. Northwestern Indians in coastal regions had as much respect for property and status as whites had. Most Indians, however, did not. The Natchez had a class structure that included a Sun God at the top and a class of 'Stinkards' at the bottom, which startled even the French. The Choctaw and Chickasaw of the Southeast were neighbors, but were enemies until the 19th century, the former being aggressive, the latter being farmers. And though the Mandan and Caddo hunted buffalo on horseback in the 19th century, they remained farmers and lived in settled villages. The rest of the Plains Indians became nomads once they got the horse. In the Southwest, the Apache roamed the deserts and mountains; the Pueblo lived in stone-built apartment blocks.

Indians differed greatly in appearance and color, and spoke hundreds of different languages belonging to some six major language groups.

Despite these differences, however, along with many others, most tribes, from the lordly Iroquois in the forests of the East to primitive tribes in the deserts of the far West, shared some things in common—beliefs that made a clash with the white man certain. It was not just the clash of Stone Age versus Industrial Age, for Indians were quick to use modern weapons and tools. It was a different view of life. Indians believed that the earth was their mother, not something that could be bought and sold and owned. The earth was a divine gift for all to share, animals as well as humans. It could be farmed for survival and hunted over and fought over, but rarely was it owned in sections like the white man owned land. Indians were close to the living world. All animals were their brothers, even those whom they hunted to survive. Indians were deeply religious and believed in 'Medicine', the spirit that protected them in everyday life and in battle.

Their communal life was indeed democratic, but democracy often led to anarchy. Indian leaders rarely had the power of white generals,

OPPOSITE TOP TO BOTTOM: Wild Horses of the American Plains *by George Catlin;* Indians Catching Wild Horses, *also by Catlin;* The Pursuit, *an 1856 engraving by N Currier. TOP LEFT: A mounted Blackfoot Indian from a painting by Carl Bodmer. TOP RIGHT: A Crow warrior painted by George Catlin. ABOVE: A Cheyenne warrior painted by the renowned western artist Frederic Remington.*

and all too often braves spoiled the effect of an attack because they were entitled to do what they wanted. Personal freedom was all-important, and it was on the warpath that a warrior was expected to make his mark.

War became faster and more exciting with the coming of the horse. By the late 18th century all Plains Indians were mounted on the de-scendants of escaped Spanish horses. Suddenly war was no longer a slogging match on foot but an almost medieval contest. It became finer to touch an enemy with a stick than kill him.

As for torture, it was common enough, especially in the East, but it was common, too, in Europe. Many tribes became more brutal because they were brutally treated by others. It should also be noted that many tribes thought well of captives, Indian or white, who could endure torture. The Iroquois and others greatly honored a prisoner who could shout or sing defiance during torture. They sometimes ate dead heroes, hoping to gain their strength.

What Indians considered utterly barbaric was prison. Joseph Brant, the great Mohawk, was appalled on a visit to England to find that

TOP LEFT: Wild rice was one of the staple crops of the Indians of Wisconsin. TOP RIGHT: The Spanish conquistadores introduced the horse to the Indians. BOTTOM ROW: Indian costumes of the 18th century. A, Mountain Indian of Hudson's Bay; B, Cree woman; C, Woman of the Wyandotte (Iroquois) tribe; D, Indian of the Mohawk tribe.

mere debtors were imprisoned. He said he would rather endure the worst tortures at the stake than imprisonment. As for scalping, though it seems to have been of Indian origin, it spread westward across the continent because of the Europeans' habit of offering bounties for scalps.

Warfare was only part of the life of even the most warlike tribe. Though an Indian woman's lot was often exhausting—women normally did the farming—children of both sexes had a wonderful time, living almost without discipline. Family life was, and is, often far closer than that of the whites. And for all the racial hatred that flared on successive frontiers as atrocity on each side was added to atrocity, many whites envied the Indians' free life, especially in early Colonial times. This view is supported by the number of captives, and not just ones taken in infancy, who preferred to stay Indian even when rescuers arrived. The frontiersmen, who

so often hated Indians, frequently lived lives not so very different from them. Indeed the true frontiersmen lost almost as much as the Indians when 'civilization' arrived. There was no place for either in a settled West—but at least the whites were not discriminated against.

Before the ancestors of today's Indians discovered the Americas some 30,000 years ago, those continents were empty of human life. Carbon-14 dating techniques have fixed the approximate time of arrival, though some new find may one day wreck current calculations. The newcomers came across what is now the Bering Strait. Even today it is only five miles

wide with islands in between. Then, during an ice age, the waters were lower and, it is thought, the strait may have been a grassy plain.

Across the plain came humans, some no doubt because of wanderlust, others because Siberia was becoming too ice-bound to support life. Whatever the reasons, they came.

North America was experiencing its own ice age, but there was a vast route free of ice east of the Rockies, and geologists have found another route farther west which could have been used as the temperature rose and the ice retreated.

Progress southward must have gone on for many centuries, possibly for 25,000 years. Latecomers, when the Bering Strait was formed, could use small boats like those of today's Eskimo to cross the water.

The greatest achievements of the descendants of the invaders were to be in Mexico and Peru. No northern Indians reached the heights of the Inca and Aztec cultures, though some had notable civilizations by the time the Euro-

TOP LEFT: Fight to the Finish *by Charles Schreyvogel.* *TOP RIGHT;* The Indian Method of Breaking a Pony *by Frederic Remington.* *ABOVE: Early Indians used dogs as beasts of burden by hitching them to travois.*

peans arrived. In fact, North America was far emptier than the rest of the hemisphere when whites first appeared in the West in 1540. Its Indian population is reckoned at between one and two million, whereas Mexico alone may have had up to 15 million people before disease and killings drastically reduced the population.

Before the Spanish arrived, the Southwest had enjoyed the golden age of the Pueblos (Spanish for towns) those bustling villages four or five stories high that were built in caverns in cliffs, on top of mesas or simply on flat ground. The great age of these experiments in communal living was from the 11th to the 13th centuries. There is a dispute as to why that age ended. Perhaps it was a combination of drought and tension in the pueblos; perhaps it was the arrival from the north of the ancestors

20

The Buffalo Dance of the Mandan Indians. In this painting by the Artist Karl Bodmer, the Indians are wearing skins and masks to work magic on one of their chief sources of food.

ABOVE: *Taos Pueblo, New Mexico.* LEFT INSET: *A battle between the Anasazi.* RIGHT INSET: *A Navajo Indian of Arizona (1910).* LEFT: *A Hopi Indian with a stick that he threw to kill rabbits.*

of the Apache and the Navaho. However, when the Spanish arrived, the area was still full of life.

They came, some of them on horses, seeking the Seven Cities of Gold. (These were the first horses the Indians had ever seen.) To the conquerors of Mexico and Peru all things seemed possible, reports of golden cities included. Instead, Francisco de Coronado and his men found villages of mud and stone that shone in the distance in the sun. Yet this expedition, which was dubbed a failure, penetrated as far as Kansas. The Grand Canyon was seen and so were the great buffalo herds; and the first wars were fought between whites and Indians in what became the United States. The Zuñi fought valiantly to defend their pueblos from the invaders with their terrible weapons—firearms and horses.

The Spaniards did not return until 1581. Then, in 1598, colonists arrived, 400 of them, and the white colonization of North America had begun. With the colonists came cattle, whose straying descendants were to be the Texas cowboys' immortal longhorns. More importantly for the Indians, horses came, whose descendants were to transform so dramatically the lives of the Plains Indians. Weapons, too, spread north and, later, spread west from the Atlantic. Firearms were obtained. Diseases were helping to reduce the number of Indians, making the white man's task far easier. Naturally, the Indians improved their weapons. Arrows soon had metal tips and firearms were obtained, but sheer numbers of men would defeat the Indians in the end, numbers that swelled as other nations reached the New World.

Spaniards had landed in the East as early as the 1530s, when several attempts were made to colonize Florida. An expedition led by a veteran of Peru, Hernando de Soto, in 1539, almost reached Oklahoma, but found no riches. Yet between them, Coronado and de Soto had almost spanned what became the United States.

TOP: A Flathead Indian mother with her child. RIGHT: A photograph of a village of the Haida People of British Columbia taken in 1890. BELOW: Pawnee Indian earth lodges on the Platte River, taken in 1870.

ABOVE: *Pueblo Indians had to be contantly on guard.* The Lookout, *by W R Leigh. Left: Sequoyah (1770?–1843), the Indian scholar who developed a Cherokee alphabet in 1821. Painting by Charles Banks Wilson.*

OPPOSITE BELOW: *Pigeon's Egg, the leader of the Assiniboine Indian tribe, painted by George Catlin.*

Before noting the other nations so soon to be on the scene, one point must be made about the Spaniards. Though their destruction of the inhabitants of the West Indies was a nightmare of human savagery, as was much of what they did in Central and South America, along with the iron-hard conquerors came noble men like Father Las Casas and his successors, who believed in Indian rights and railed against their oppressors. Thanks to them, the enslavement of Indians was banned, and even proud conquistadors could be tried for cruelty. Of course, the human misery went on, but the Spanish record is shot through with beacons of light and humanity. Humanity was not to be much in evidence among the Anglo-Americans.

LEFT: Indians Fishing from a Canoe in North Carolina, *painted by John White, probably in 1585.*

ABOVE: *A lithograph by Karl Bodmer showing some teepees of the Assiniboine Tribe of Indians.*

BELOW: *A photograph of 20th century Zuñi Indians of New Mexico performing a Rain Dance.*

OPPOSITE PAGE: *The Zuñis, a tribe of Pueblo Indians, also had their Buffalo Dances. This print, made in 1854, shows a Zuñi brave costumed to begin a dance.*

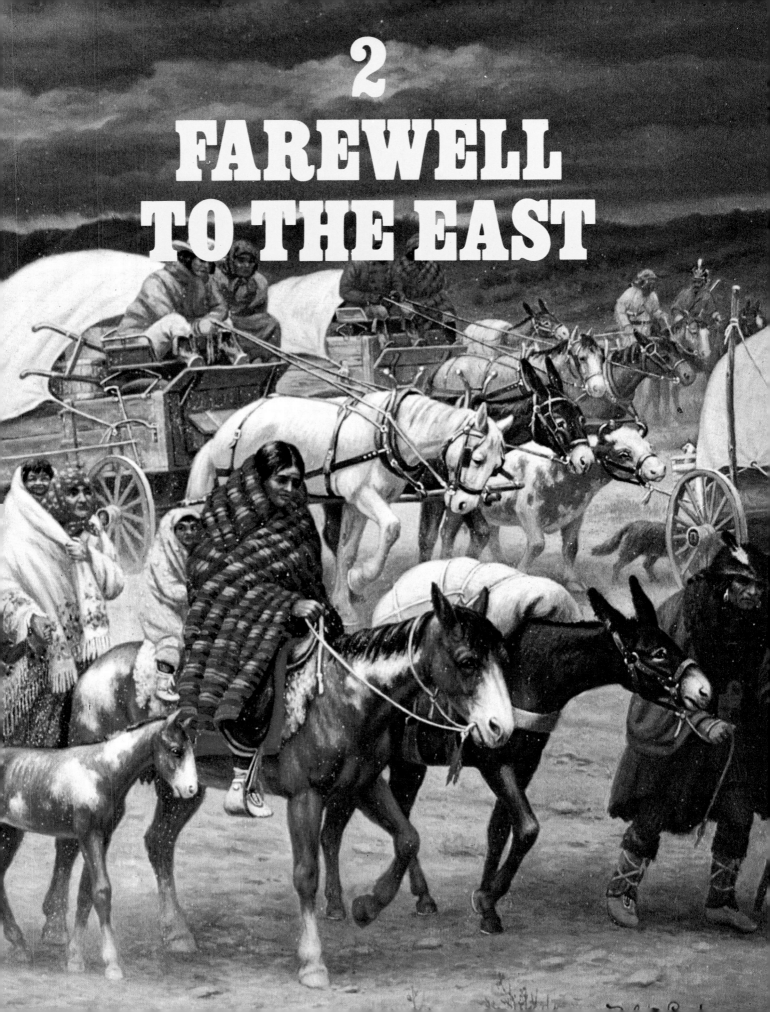

2
FAREWELL
TO THE EAST

'When I passed the last detachment of those suffering exiles and thought that my native countrymen had thus expelled them from their native soil and their much loved homes, and that too in this inclement season of the year, I turned from the sight with feelings which language cannot express and "wept like childhood then." '

So wrote 'A Native of Maine' in a New York paper in 1839 about his glimpse of the Cherokee on their journey to Indian Territory, leaving their beloved homeland forever. In all, some 60,000 Indians of the Five Civilized Tribes—Cherokee, Creek, Choctaw, Chickasaw and Seminoles—were exiled in a series of Trails of Tears, a direct result of a frontiersman, Andrew Jackson, being elected President in 1828. Here is how it happened.

The story of the Indians repeated itself down the centuries: the arrival of the white man, often welcomed; growing tensions, usually over land; the wars which whites almost always won in the end; and disease, liquor and despair. No doubt the ancestors of that undeniably humane man from Maine had been less emotional when it came to clearing Indians from the Atlantic seaboard in the north.

The French record is the best, for they were principally interested in the fur trade, not in land or in colonization. They married Indian women. Both trappers and priests learned Indian languages. Two years before the first English colony was established at Jamestown, Virginia in 1607, a French trading post was set up at Port Royal, Acadia (now Nova Scotia). The place was chosen by Samuel de Champlain, one of New France's (Canada's) greatest heroes. In the end, New France fell to the English because of lack of troops and lack of support from home, but Champlain hardly helped matters by making an enemy of the mighty Iroquois Confederacy.

The Iroquois were rightly feared warriors, but they also had a remarkable gift for democratic government, much admired by Benjamin Franklin and other Americans. The Five Nations of the Confederacy (the Mohawk, Oneida, Onondaga, Cayuga and Seneca) lived in a key position in western and central New York, an area rich in waterways which enabled them to dominate the fur trade and to be courted by Europeans. In the 18th century they became the Six Nations, giving a home to the Tuscarora, who were suffering from the oppression of whites in the Carolinas.

Champlain turned the Iroquois against France when, with two other Frenchmen, he was out with a Huron war party. His object was exploration, but the Huron were enemies of the Iroquois and a clash with a band of Mohawk was won by the Frenchmen's use of firearms, which killed three chiefs. This led to enduring hostility between the French and the Iroquois, with few periods of neutrality. Hostility grew worse when captive Iroquois were sent to be galley slaves in the Mediterranean. The Iroquois alliance with the English, a reasonably constant one, had its beginnings in that small forest incident.

To the south, the English colony of Jamestown managed to survive a series of crises and disasters, not least because of the aid given by the enchanting young Indian woman, Pocahontas. Not only did she save the life of the colony's most determined leader, Captain John Smith, when her father Powhatan was about to have him killed (some cynics believe that Smith made up the story) but also by marrying John Rolfe and becoming the ancestor of many distinguished Americans, she decisively helped the two races to coexist. Sad to say, she died in England, just as she was about to return home from her triumphs at the Court of King James I and elsewhere.

Soon the Indians found themselves under more and more pressure from the English, primarily because tobacco, the key crop being raised, used up land quickly and more was needed. So a reasonably harmonious atmosphere, especially among the older settlers, was transformed into hostility which led to war. Too late, the Powhatans rebelled in 1622. Already the colonists' population had swelled enough to take a terrible revenge on the Indians whose numbers had been reduced by disease.

Meanwhile, two years earlier the Pilgrim Fathers had landed to the north on Cape Cod. Intensely religious, they were helped by the local Indians, without whom they might have starved. The same basic sequence of events oc-

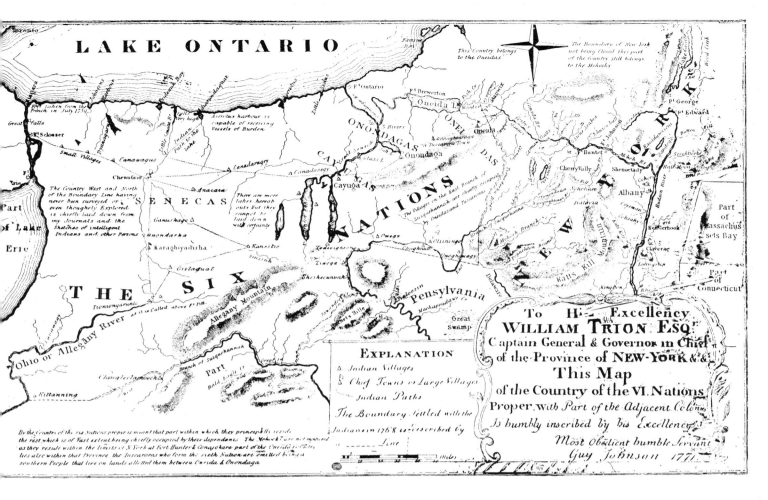

ABOVE: *A map of 1771 by Guy Johnson showing the territory of the Six (Indian) Nations of the Confederacy.*

RIGHT: *An old print of Champlain attacking an Indian village.* BELOW RIGHT: *Champlain attacking an Iroquois fort.*

curred, the war in this case, 'King Philip's War,' breaking out in 1675. After the defeat of the Indian confederacy led by Metacom, King Philip, of the Wampanoag, hundreds of Indians were sent as slaves to the West Indies, including Philip's wife and child. That child was the grandson of the 'noble Massasoit' who had done so much to help the Pilgrims. Reverend Increase Mather, some of whose sayings on the subject of the Indian dead deserve a place in an anthology of bestiality, made one significant statement about what Philip's reaction must have been on hearing about the capture of his family: 'It must be bitter as death for him to lose his wife and only son, for the Indians are marvellously fond and affectionate towards their children.'

Philip was killed soon after the loss of his family. As for Mather's gleeful remark, the chief is said to have exclaimed on hearing the

32

news of his loss: 'My heart breaks; now I am ready to die . . .'

During the holocaust unleashed by the Indians, Rogers Williams of Rhode Island, who had been banished from Massachusetts for championing religious tolerance and, equally out-of-line, Indian land rights, was spared, along with his colony. He and William Penn, who made a treaty with the Delaware in 1682, were famous exceptions to the rule of hostility. Yet many ordinary whites and Indians, even in desperate times, enjoyed genuine friendships.

The Dutch proved that they could commit atrocities as heinous as any. On Staten Island in 1643, where Wappinger who had asked for protection were slaughtered, a Hackensack was tortured in front of a laughing governor in a manner that equalled the Iroquois at their cruelest. The victim was even fed his own flesh. Fiendish as Indian torture could be, they at least had respect for the valiant.

There was never any real hope of the Indians throwing the whites into the Atlantic except, perhaps, in the earliest days. The settlers would

LEFT: *Pocahontas (also known as Matoaks) in London, 1616.* BELOW: *A statue of the chief of the Wampanoag, Massasoit, located in Plymouth, Massachusetts.*

have come again anyway. However, in the 1760s there was a rebellion that might have driven the English back to the coast for a time, at least.

The French had by now lost Canada. Too few in numbers, they had long ago lost their main Indian allies, the Huron, who had been destroyed as a major power by the Iroquois in 1649.

Before the French and Indian War (known as the Seven Years' War in Canada) broke out in 1756, the Indians and some Frenchmen had won a devastating victory against General Braddock's army in the forests of Pennsylvania. This was followed by other successes, but Wolfe's victory at Quebec in 1759 and Amherst's at Montreal in 1760 saw the end of New France.

One reason for the British victory was the refusal once again of the Iroquois to help the French. They stayed loyal partly because of the skill of William Johnson. This genial Irishman liked acquiring land but also genuinely liked Indians. As trader, then as 'Colonel of the Six

RIGHT: Joseph Brant (also known as Thayendanegea), chief of the Mohawk Indians, 1776.
BELOW: Osceola, the chief of the Seminole Indians of Florida.

Nations', finally as superintendent of all Indian affairs in the north, he was one of the most influential men in America. He became Sir William for his services at the Battle of Lake George in 1755, Britain's only victory that grim year, achieved by some 3000 Colonists and 300 Iroquois, mostly Mohawk. Johnson's charm even disarmed the fanatically religious New Englanders, when, before the battle, he did a war dance with his Indian friends. Yet it was all even he could do to keep the Iroquois loyal when the Ottawa chief, Pontiac, led his rebellion in 1763. In fact, the Seneca, the most westerly tribe of the Iroquois, joined Pontiac for a time.

Pontiac's aim was to bring back the French as well as drive the English back over the Alleghenies. Fort after fort fell to the Indians, who, just for once, were truly united. But the fort at Detroit held, and Pontiac gradually lost control of his many different tribes. The great rebellion faded and collapsed.

Now, with the French menace ended, it was only a matter of time before the Colonists rebelled against England, whose policies were guaranteed to provoke rebellion. Yet on the frontier, Britain's policy was honorable. There was a genuine attempt to keep Americans out of Indian territory. They drew the Proclamation Line of 1763, which aimed to keep the Colonists east of the watershed of the Alleghenies. But it infuriated both Virginian land companies and the growing number of people who wished to head westward.

When the American Revolution broke out in 1775, both sides trying to enlist Indian aid, the British having more success, probably because Sir William Johnson had died the previous year. Now, though his son, Sir John, and other members of his family, were key members of the Loyalist side in New York, the leading figure on the northern frontier was Joseph Brant (Thayendanegea) the war chief of the Six Nations.

Brant was the younger brother of Molly Brant, Johnson's last Mohawk mistress, regarded, however, by everyone as his wife. Frontier opinion, and portraits, suggest that Brant may have been Johnson's son by another Indian woman, and Sir William certainly saw

to it that he was well educated. As a youth he had fought in the French and Indian War; now he was the leading Indian figure in New York. Even his influence could not prevent the Iroquois, the Tuscarora, and the Oneida from siding mainly with the Rebels, the Onondaga remaining generally neutral. Brant went to London in 1775–76 to be sure that a British alliance would safeguard Indian land rights. Boswell interviewed him, Romney painted him, and he made a deep impression on all who met him. Satisfied, he returned to America, fought on Long Island where he made a lifelong friend in Lord Hugh Percy, later second Duke of Northumberland and an honorary Mohawk, then penetrated north to his people.

Though many tribes fought with the British in the war, only Brant and his Iroquois had it in their power to change its course. The fertile Mohawk valley, once Brant's home, was Washington's army's breadbasket, and the Indians and Tory Loyalists virtually destroyed it. The hardiest of the surviving settlers hung on until Washington had troops to spare to ravage the Iroquois homeland. But the final blow came when the Iroquois were left out of the peace treaty of 1783. They split, some remained in New York, and Brant led the rest to the Grand River in what is now Ontario, where today their descendants live just outside Brantford. Brant paid an even more spectacular visit to London in 1786, once again to secure his people's rights. Like Pontiac, and like Tecumseh after him, he had a vision of an Indian front united against the Americans, but he had to content himself with his smaller world in Canada, where, as an Iroquois and an officer in the British Army, his loyalties were divided. President Washington personally offered him generous rewards to help effect peace in the Northwest, but American peace usually meant loss of Indian land. The offer was rejected.

Finally, after the United States Army had been utterly defeated on the northern frontier in 1791 and 1792, the Americans won a great victory at Fallen Timbers in 1794. Now the days of the Indians in the Northwest were numbered.

Early in the nineteenth century, the great Shawnee, Tecumseh, became the last to try to

ABOVE LEFT: *Iroquois warriors attacking American settlers in their cabin.* BELOW LEFT: *American colonists warding off another Iroquois attack.* ABOVE: *Seventeenth century combat between an Indian and a settler.*

unite the eastern tribes and hold the border, which was then the Ohio River. A magnificent orator and a man of rare stature and vision, his power over many different tribes had the Americans genuinely worried. Once again it seemed that the Indians might be truly united. General William Henry Harrison, governor of Indiana and a notable procurer of Indian lands, recognized the danger, but in 1811, when Tecumseh was absent, his messianic brother, known as the Prophet, launched a premature attack on Harrison at Tippecanoe which failed. He was discredited and Tecumseh's union was doomed. The next year, he decided to side with the British in the War of 1812. He helped destroy American chances of seizing Canada, but was killed at the Battle of the Thames in 1813. After that, the idea of a single united Indian nation, always an impossible dream, crumbled away forever.

By the 1830s, with the sad campaign called Black Hawk's War, the Indians were finally driven westward, the only ones left in the old Northwest being a few scattered bands located around the Great Lakes. Tribes, some still re-membered, some of them forgotten, had fought and had lost and were banished from the East forever, tribes whose very names—Delaware, Miami and the rest—are like tunes of vanished glories.

The most notorious of all these enforced removals were those of the Five Civilized Tribes. They had a long and complicated relationship with the white powers—England, Spain, France and, finally, the United States—which tried to dominate the South. They had often fought against each other. Their civilizations advanced swiftly in the early years of the 19th century, none more so than that of the Cherokee. Their government was modeled on the

United States government, while thanks to Sequoya's alphabet, the Cherokee rapidly became literate, even publishing a newspaper in 1828. Their chief was the remarkable John Ross, totally identified with them, though only one-eighth Indian.

The Creeks, too, had an extraordinary leader, Alexander McGillivray, at a time when the Creek and Seminoles were one nation. He died in 1796, having established himself as a diplomat of genius in his crafty dealings with Americans, British and Spaniards. Andrew Jackson, who had been well served by Indian troops in his time, and whose lands he then managed to reduce, started work on his Indian Removal Bill almost as soon as he became President in 1828. It needed the cooperation of the states concerned to facilitate his plans, but Georgia, Alabama and Mississippi were only too eager to help. The Cherokee, by now some of the most prosperous citizens in the United States, were well and truly doomed when gold was found on their land. The matter reached the Supreme Court and John Marshall, the Chief Justice, decided that Georgia had no right to the Cherokee lands. He spoke passionately, but Jackson said:

'John Marshall has made his decision; now let him enforce it.'

So it came about that the Five Civilized Tribes were herded to Indian Territory, the amount of cruelty involved in these Trails of Tears varying from place to place and tribe to tribe. At their worst they shamed humanity. It is absurd to misunderstand the reason for anti-Indian feeling on the frontier, especially when the wars were at their height and atrocity was breeding atrocity, but these tribes in the 1830s were much more admirable citizens than most of those who wanted them out. Only the Seminoles, helped by the place they chose for their heroic stand, the Everglades of Florida, put up serious resistance to the inevitable.

The First Seminole War (1816–18) took place when Florida was still Spanish. Runaway slaves fled there and joined the Indians. Jackson marched in, defeated the Indians and prepared the ground for Florida's incorporation into the Union. The Second Seminole War (1835–42) broke out when the Indians refused to go west. Hellish for the troops involved, the war was an epic of endurance, even by Indian standards. While a few unfortunate Indians

CHEROKEE ALPHABET.

CHARACTERS SYSTEMATICALLY ARRANGED WITH THE SOUNDS

D	R	T	Ꮤ	Oᵒ	i
a	e	i	o	oo	v
ga ka	ge	gi	go	gu	gv
ha	he	hi	ho	hu	hv
la	le	li	lo	lu	lv
ma	me	mi	mo	mu	
na hna nah	ne	ni	no	nu	nv
qua	que	qni	quo	quu	quv
s sa	se	si	so	su	sv
da ta	de te	di ti	do	du	dv
dla tla	tle	tli	tlo	tlu	tlv
tsa	tse	tsi	tso	tsu	tsv
wa	we	wi	wo	wu	wv
ya	ye	yi	yo	yu	yv

SOUNDS REPRESENTED BY VOWELS

A as a in father, or short as a in rival.
E as a in hate, or short as e in met.
I as i in pique, or short as i in pin.
O as o in note, but as approaching to aw in law.
U as oo in moon, or short as u in pull.
V as u in but, nasalized.

CONSONANT SOUNDS.

G, is sounded hard approaching to k; sometimes before e, i, u and v, its sound is k. D has a sound between the English d and t; sometimes, before o, u, and v its sound is t; when written before l and s the same analogy prevails
All other letters as in English.
Syllables beginning with g, except ga have sometimes the power of k; syllables when written with tl, except tla sometimes vary to dla.

were taken to Indian Territory when captured, the rest, under Osceola, a chief of storybook nobility, kept up a ferocious struggle against soldiers, sailors and bloodhounds. At a conference in 1835, Osceola was treacherously seized, and he died in prison. His comrade Wild Cat, with 16 warriors and two women, made an incredible escape from the fort at St Augustine through a small hole 18 feet from the floor. Meanwhile, in the Everglades mothers killed their small children so as to fight with the men.

Finally, the Americans had had enough. Those Seminoles who wanted to stay were allowed to do so. Some, without actually fighting, remained officially at war with the United States, and not until 1962 did they resume relations with the nation that failed to defeat them.

One other group survives to this day in the East. A few hundred Cherokee escaped one of the Trails of Tears by hiding out in the mountains of North Carolina. Their descendants— some 4500 of them—have not intermarried with other groups, unlike the Cherokee of Oklahoma. In a special amphitheater in their beautiful reservation, visitors can see the most famous of all dramas staged by Indians about their past, *Unto These Hills*. For the Cherokee of North Carolina, unlike so many of today's Indians, past and present are happily united.

OPPOSITE TOP LEFT: The death of Tecumseh, the Shawnee Indian chief (1768–1813).
OPPOSITE BOTTOM LEFT: The defeat of the Sac and the Fox in the Battle of Bad Axe.
OPPOSITE RIGHT: A Virginia Indian village of 1590.
ABOVE: Sequoya's Cherokee alphabet, 1821.
RIGHT: John Ross, a leader of the Cherokee Indians.

A painting by Charles M Russell showing some Comanche Indian braves returning from a horse stealing raid.

3
FAR WESTERN TRAGEDY

'Gold! Gold! Gold from the American River!' That cry, shouted in the main street of the small town of San Francisco on 15 May, 1848 by an extrovert Mormon named Sam Brannan, gave away the secret of James Marshall's gold strike at Sutter's Mill the previous January. It was a cry that was to reverberate round the world, bring hundreds of thousands of people to California, and spell the doom of its Indians.

California, so soon to be known as the Golden State, had a larger Indian population than any other area of similar size in North America. In terms of art, agriculture and social organization, the vast number of small groups seen by Europeans from the 16th century onward were among the least developed of all Indians. Though some of those who lived in the deserts of Utah and Nevada were still less developed. Yet California's Indians seem to have been happy enough. There was no shortage of food and the climate varied from pleasant to idyllic. Only the Mohave and the Yuma who lived in the southeastern region were in the least organized, and only the Yuma were farmers. The rest led a mainly peaceful and dreamlike existence. The few visitors from European ships found the natives they met both friendly and happy.

Not until 1769 did Spain move into California—Upper California as it was known then. A Russian threat from the north was the reason for the migration. Along with garrisons came the famous Californian missions, 21 of them in all, staffed by Franciscan priests.

Considering what was to happen later, the missions stand out as the reasonably humane institutions they were certainly meant to be. But in fact, only the coastal Indians were influenced by the missions, and, instead of their old, carefree life, they found themselves working hard at every sort of trade, including outdoor activities like farming, which must have seemed singularly pointless. The priests tried to turn them into good Catholics, punished them with the lash if they misbehaved, and let them out occasionally in groups to collect fruit and potential converts. Many of the priests were fine, dedicated men, but they were at best benevolent despots as far as their charges were concerned. Laughing faces became sullen. The missions succeeded but their workers lost that simple happiness noticed by earlier travelers.

What would have happened if Spain had remained the ruler of California can only be guessed at. It would certainly have been infinitely better for the Indians than what did happen.

Mexico broke away from Spain in 1821 and the missions were made secular in 1834. At least the Indians had had security under the Spanish priests, but now the Mexican liberators grabbed the missions and the spoils in a way Henry VIII would have recognized, with the result that huge ranchos were formed.

Already the Indian population was shrinking. From 1800 to 1850, it slumped from 260,000 to 100,000. This was not deliberate genocide—that came later—but was simply caused by new diseases and new ways of life. Even the conquest of California by Americans in 1846 was not in itself a prelude to disaster, but the finding of gold on the American River was; and ironically, it was found just over a week before the official peace treaty between Mexico and the United States made California American.

A single statistic without embellishment sums up the story. By 1900, there were only 15,000 Indians left alive in California. It is reckoned that as early as 1859 there were only 30,000 left.

Only a minority of the many thousands of whites from the eastern United States and other parts of the world who poured into California had the remotest interest in, or sympathy for, the native population. And it hardly helped the Indians that, unlike so many tribes elsewhere, they were nearly all peace-loving with no warrior tradition. The southern Californian Indians, far from the goldfields, suffered less, in the sense that many of them survived in however debauched a state. But further north, Indians were hunted down like animals, killed or enslaved, their women raped and often forced into prostitution, their children brought up in bondage. The only reason that they were not wiped out altogether was that there were too many of them. The map of California is dotted with small reservations where some of their descendants live today.

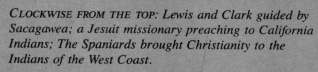

CLOCKWISE FROM THE TOP: Lewis and Clark guided by Sacagawea; a Jesuit missionary preaching to California Indians; The Spaniards brought Christianity to the Indians of the West Coast.

There was only one genuine war in California, fought along the border with Oregon. It was a valiant one, but marred by a brutal, foolish murder at a time when the Indians concerned needed all the moral support they could get.

These Indians were the Modoc. They lived in the Tule Lake country, and in the 1850s they found their best land being annexed by the whites. Unlike so many Californian Indians, the Modoc were prepared to fight back, but a young chief called Kintpuash decided to try and get along with the intruders. He liked their way of life, and the two races settled down on reasonably amicable terms. The Americans gave a number of the Modoc new names, Kintpuash acquiring the name by which he is remembered today—Captain Jack.

In the Civil War period, relations deteriorated and the whites managed to get the Modoc moved to the Klamath Reservation in Oregon, where they found themselves regarded as interlopers. Worse, supplies reached the Klamath from the government, but none came for the Modoc. So Captain Jack and his people went home. The authorities there were prepared to allow them to stay, but the local settlers were not. Naturally, evil reports were circulated about Jack and his people, and, finally, the tribe was ordered to return to Oregon. In November, 1872, Captain James Jackson at the head of B Troop, First Cavalry, headed out of Fort Klamath for the Modoc home on Lost River.

A tense confrontation occurred, with Jackson ordering Captain Jack and his men to lay down their arms. They did so, with the exception of Scarface Charley (another white nickname), who drew his pistol on Jackson. Both men fired and both were unharmed. Meanwhile the Modoc rushed for their pile of arms and a fight commenced, ending after half an hour with the flight of the Indians. Jackson claimed that 'not

less than 16' of the 'worst' of them were dead, though, in fact, only one was, as was one of his own men.

The families of Jack's band paddled along the river leading to Lake Tule while their men marched along the bank. The band led by Hooker Jim was attacked by ranchers, who were beaten back, and the two groups met each other in lava beds below the lake, which were to be known as Captain Jack's Stronghold, and which are now a National Monument.

This natural fortress, well known to the Indians, had just enough grass for the cattle the Modoc brought with them, while the lake would provide water. Into the fortress came some 250 Modoc, probably not more than 60 of them warriors. Captain Jack was alarmed that Hooker Jim had killed local whites whom the Indians knew. He had hoped to be left in peace in the stronghold, but realized that war was now inevitable.

The soldiers arrived on 13 January 1873 and a reconnaissance party was driven away from a bluff. On the 16th, 225 regulars and 104 volunteers appeared. It seems that Jack decided there was no point in fighting if it meant the destruction of his people, but he was outvoted. Naturally, those who had killed settlers wanted no surrender.

The first attack, complete with artillery, started the next day. It ended in failure, and the Indians went out and collected guns and ammunition from the dead. The whites rightly decided that they needed more troops and guns.

The commander of the Department of the Columbia, General Canby, a humane and popular man, came to take personal control of the embarrassing little war. Already there had been peace feelers, carried to Jack by his cousin Winema, who was married to a white man, Frank Riddle. The Americans were offering a reservation in the Southwest, away from possible trial in a hostile Oregon. Hooker Jim was so impressed that he and eight followers actually surrendered to the peace commissioners. These were Alfred Meacham, once the Modoc agent in Oregon, L S Dyar from the Klamath Reservation, and Reverend Eleasar Thomas, a Methodist. Unfortunately, an Oregonian spotted the Modoc, made some pointed remarks about the dead settlers, and the Indians escaped as fast as they could to the safety of the stronghold.

Jack was soon in an intolerable situation, for it was announced that he and his band could come in safety, but that Hooker Jim and his men could not. Despite a friendly meeting with Canby, more and more troops arrived. By April there were to be 1000 of them. Canby kept trying to resolve the crisis peacefully and several meetings took place in no-man's-land, but al-

LEFT: A scene of an Indian family on the move. The horses at the right are pulling travois loaded with household goods. OPPOSITE BELOW: A maiden of the Blackfoot tribe, painted by N H Hardy. RIGHT: The Whitman Mission in 1845. BELOW: A Comanche warrior as painted by George Catlin.

ways the question of Hooker Jim and his men prevented a solution from being found.

After one bitter council in the stronghold, Winema, sent in by Canby to tell Jack that any who wished to surrender to him could come out with her, was stopped by a relative. He warned her that Hooker Jim's faction was prepared to kill anyone who opposed them, including white men, at any future meeting. Her husband passed on the warning to the peace commissioners, but it was written off as a mere threat. Hooker Jim, however, meant what he said. At the climax of another angry council, he told Jack that unless he killed Canby at their next meeting, he would be killed by his own people. Jack told him it would be the act of a coward to kill Canby, but Hooker Jim said it would be a brave act in front of the soldiers. Women's clothes were draped over Jack's shoulders and he was jeered at and disowned by his opponents, who later were so foully to betray him. Finally, he gave in and said he would kill the general.

An English-speaking Modoc, Boston Charley, went to Canby and asked for a meeting to be held on 11 April—Good Friday. The Modoc would be unarmed and so should the commissioners be.

Jack made one more plea to his opponents, but was outvoted again. Finally, they decided that if Canby would agree to the Modoc terms, he would not be killed. The terms were the granting of a reservation nearby and the removal of the troops before peace talks. Jack had told the council what would happen if Canby were killed, but it made no difference. The countdown to tragedy had begun.

The council tent stood midway between the stronghold and the headquarters of Colonel Gillem, First Cavalry. It had been erected a few days earlier in case of sudden storms. The Indians arrived first: Jack, Hooker Jim, and four other Modoc, all with pistols under their coats. They built a sagebrush fire, as the day was chilly. Then the commissioners arrived: Canby, Thomas, Meacham, and Dyar, also Frank Riddle and Winema, who was known as Toby to the whites. Riddle was Canby's official interpreter. With them also were Boston Charley and Bogus Charley, who had been sent ahead to the white men's camp. They both had rifles over their shoulders; Dyar and Meacham carried concealed derringers.

Canby made a friendly speech, promising a good country where the Modoc could live like white people. Jack said he did not want to leave the Modoc country, but live on a reservation between the lake and the lava beds. Also the soldiers must go away before any peace talks.

Meacham now said that any Modoc who wanted to, could stay in the lava beds until a new reservation was found, while Hooker Jim took Meacham's coat from his saddle and donned it, saying: 'You think I look like Meacham.' To lower the tension, Meacham offered his hat as well. 'You keep a while,' said Hooker Jim. 'Hat will be mine by and by.'

Canby pointed out that only the President could send the troops away. After a few more exchanges, Jack suddenly shouted in Modoc: 'All ready,' drew his pistol and killed Canby. Boston Charley killed Thomas, but Meacham was saved when Winema knocked the pistol aside. The other commissioner, Dyar, escaped with the Riddles. General Sherman wired Canby's immediate superior, General Schofield: 'Any measure of severity to the savages will be sustained.' He had the nation behind him. Meanwhile, Colonel Gillem, with Canby's death the senior officer on the spot, began working his way toward the stronghold, the attacks beginning on 15 April with a new, grim earnestness. On the third day, the troops entered the stronghold only to find that the enemy had vanished.

Terino Indian scouts found them again, but the 64-strong army reconnaissance force that went in to check their new defensive position was humiliatingly ambushed. Half the patrol ran away and of the courageous rest, 25 were killed and 16 were wounded.

OPPOSITE PAGE: *Probably the greatest leader of the Nez Percé Indian tribe—Chief Joseph (1840?–1904).*

INSET: *Another photograph of Chief Joseph at the end of his career. His Indian name was Hinmaton-Yalatkit, or Thunder Rolling in the Mountains.*

The new commander, General Jefferson C Davis, made some strong remarks about the quality of his enlisted men, but he was an able commander, and by mid-May, he had more troops and had managed to raise the morale of his shaky command. However, when he moved in on the Modoc positions, the enemy had vanished once more.

This was not a strategic withdrawal by a united force. The Modoc had broken up into small bands. Hooker Jim with 13 men and their families had deserted the leader whose inevitable destruction he had caused, then, despicably, he surrendered to Davis and offered to find Jack in return for amnesty. The turncoats tracked down Jack and urged him to surrender. He told them to go back to the whites. If they came near him, he would shoot them like curs. But, finally and inevitably, he was caught, dressed in what was left of Canby's uniform. 'Jack's legs gave out,' he said. 'I am ready to die.'

After a trial in language they little understood, Captain Jack, Schonchin John, Boston Charley and Black Jim were hanged. Hooker Jim was one of those who gave evidence against them.

Jack's courage held to the end. When a settler shouted to him as the rope was being adjusted round his neck: 'Jack! What would you give me to take your place?', he flashed back: '500 ponies and both my wives!'

Jack's body was dug up the night after the hanging and was soon appearing in the East at carnivals at 10 cents a look.

Robert A Murray, historian of the Modoc War, notes that considering the number of Indians involved in hostilities, this was the most expensive Indian war that the United States ever fought. It was also the only war in which an army general was killed by Indians.

One hundred fifty-three Modoc were sent to Indian Territory, where Hooker Jim died. In 1909, those survivors who wished to, were allowed to return to the Northwest and settle on the Klamath Reservation in Oregon.

An additional casualty of the expensive and humiliating war was President Grant's Peace Policy. This dated back to 1868 and advocated the concentration of Indians, civilizing and educating them, and getting them to become self-sufficient in feeding themselves. The war, especially the slaying of Canby and Thomas, made the very word peace suspect, despite the fact that the causes of the war had precious little to do with anything but local white mismanagement of and hostility toward a small group of people. In the public and official mind, however, it was now even more fully established that Indians could not be trusted. As a result, such peace policy as there was became to signify peace for Indians on the reservation and war for those off it.

In the Great Basin country of Nevada and Utah, between the Sierra Nevada and the Rockies, lived peoples whose life-styles were even simpler than those of California's Indians. Most spoke variations of the Shoshonean language, and some, like the Gosiute, or Diggers, beside the Great Salt Lake, were perhaps the most primitive Indians in America. Yet cousins of these desert dwellers, the Shoshones of Wyoming, led the stirring life of the Plains Indians.

OPPOSITE: *Tomochichi of the Yamacraw Creek Indians with his son.* ABOVE: *A Blackfoot Indian youth undergoing the ordeal of the Sun Dance — a ritual which he must suffer in order to become a warrior.*

There were Ute in Utah and Colorado, Paiute on the Nevada-Utah border; there were Bannock—mountain Paiute—in Idaho, and Klamath, whom we have already briefly met, in Oregon, and a wealth of tribes in northern Oregon and Washington. Above all, there were the Nez Percé.

The Diggers were too poor to cause anyone much trouble, and their land was too barren for them to be exterminated on account of it. They therefore remained. The Paiute were more daring. A frontier mob, 105 strong, whose slogan was 'An Indian for breakfast and a pony to ride', attacked Paiute at Pyramid Lake after an incident which seems to have begun with the raping of two Indian women. The Indians won, but, as inevitably happened, lost the short war that followed. Otherwise, the main Paiute claim to historical fame is their racing after Pony Express riders.

The Northern Shoshones have a greater claim to fame. The Comanche, the lords of the south plains, were a breakaway branch of the tribe, but the Shoshones who remained were famous in their own right. Lewis and Clark's much admired guide, Sacagawea, was a Shoshone. Arguments have raged as to how useful—as opposed to how delightful—she was, but the fact that Lewis and Clark had an Indian woman with them on their great expedition to the Pacific and back (1804–06) undoubtedly helped allay the fears of watching Indians, and she was able to be of considerable service when she reached her own tribe; she had been kidnapped from them some years earlier. The Shoshones helped the party head westward.

Later, the Shoshones, under their great Chief Washakie, who died in his nineties in 1900, were to be good friends of the whites. They helped settlers and—thanks to their long hostility to the Sioux and Cheyenne—helped the army on the plains. For that, certain writers have dubbed them mercenaries in the less pleasant sense of the word. In fact, they were allies against a common enemy and it is unhistorical to suggest otherwise, even if the 'hostiles' are now more widely admired by Indians and white men alike. The Pawnee served the whites for exactly the same reason.

The Indians of the Northwest—Joseph and his Nez Percé apart—are not often treated at any length except in specialized books. Only a few can be described here, yet their fate was as wretched as that of most tribes. They had obtained horses around 1700, and many lived along the Columbia River and its tributaries. The Yakima, who were also called Cayuse, became famous horse dealers—so much so that Oregonians started calling horses cayuses, and the term later spread through the West.

Though the great emigrations to Oregon did not start until 1843, they were originally triggered off by the reports of missionaries in Oregon, most notably the Methodist, Dr Jason Lee in 1834, and the Congregational minister, Dr Marcus Whitman in 1836. The thousands of Americans who crossed the plains and mountains made the Northwest American, not British as it might have been, by right of possession. War-like noises were made by President Polk that the border between Canada and the United States be drawn at the 54th Parallel, but in 1846, it was settled at the 49th.

At first, there was little trouble between the Indians and the newcomers. There were only some 10,000 of them by the end of the 1840s, not to be compared in numbers or in character with the flood of Forty-Niners so soon to overwhelm California's tribes.

Whitman and his wife, Narcissa, settled with the Cayuse at their request. Their mission was near today's Walla Walla in southern Washington. The other missionaries, the Spaldings and William Gray, settled with the Nez Percé at Lapwai in Idaho.

After a good start, and with other missionaries coming West to join them, problems started to arise: a money shortage back in the East, a troublemaking missionary called Smith, and conversions to Catholicism being made by priests coming down from Hudson's Bay Com-

OPPOSITE ABOVE: Two Digger, or Paiute, Indians of Nevada. BELOW: Beavers were important to Indians as sources of both fur and food. This is the culmination of a beaver hunt.

pany posts. 'Romanism stalks abroad,' said Mrs. Spalding. Its finest figure was Father de Smet, the Jesuit who spent many years with the Flathead and Coeur d'Alene Indians in Montana.

With the Protestant missions being threatened with closure—their officials in the East soon changed their minds—Whitman went back to report, returning with the great wagon train of 1843. Tension grew each year, and the Spaldings had to close their once successful mission school, partly because a Delaware who had married a Nez Percé was violently antimissionary. He felt this way because of the way his people had been treated in the East. Christianity seemed to him a sham.

The school closed in 1846 and that winter was a very severe one. Cruelly, the Cayuse suffered several hundred deaths from measles, many deaths being perhaps caused by their drastic attempt at a cure—a steam bath followed by a dip in cold water. Rumors spread that Whitman was poisoning Indians to take their lands, that missionaries and settlers were in league to that same end. The conversion battle between Catholics and Protestants hardly helped.

On 29 November 1847, the Cayuse struck the Whitman mission. It was a typically busy day. There were now many white assistants, also workers and children. Dr and Mrs Whitman were killed along with eleven other men, and women and children were taken prisoner, including the daughters of mountain men Jim Bridger and Joe Meek. Both girls, whose mothers were Indian, had measles and died of exposure.

Only the bravery of Mrs. Spalding and the good faith of a Nez Percé chief prevented another massacre at Lapwai. Though no friend of missionaries, the chief and his men helped the whites to escape.

Volunteers joined some Regulars to punish the Cayuse, and in 1850, to save the rest of the tribe, five of the Indians turned themselves in, after two years of hiding in the mountains.

California Indian women sorting acorns that have been brought in from the forests—painting by A A Jansson.

They were hanged. As so often happened, the wrong people—in this case, well-meaning friends of the Indians—had been attacked by those who rightly saw their way of life being threatened. And they had unwittingly chosen the worst possible time, with the country soon to be invaded by hordes of ex-Forty-Niners hoping to strike it rich further north. Worse still, Washington became a separate territory in 1853 under the governorship of a tough ex-army man, Isaac Stevens.

He was a keen railroad advocate—on his way to his new job he conducted a War Department Pacific Railway Survey—and he was soon pushing the idea of a northern transcontinental line. This, of course, would mean getting rid of awkward Indian land titles. After several small tribes west of the Cascade Mountains had been moved to reservations, he arranged for a major council to be held at Walla Walla. All the Indians of the upper Columbia River country who had had little or no contact with whites, were to attend.

The Council was held in May 1855 and the Indians were understandably suspicious. They had heard of the 'war' against the Rogue River Indians of southern Oregon waged by volunteers in 1853, which ended in the valley being 'bought' from the Indians for a trivial sum. In fact, the year after the Walla Walla Council, the Rogue River Indians were to rise again and be almost exterminated.

At Walla Walla were Yakima under their outstanding Chief Kamiakim, who had been trying to unite the tribes before the council started. There were also Nez Percé, Cayuse, Walla Walla and Umatilla. Stevens wanted them all to be placed on two reservations with the Nez Percé and Yakima. This idea was firmly rejected. Finally, after much bitter negotiating, vast areas of land were ceded by the Indians in return for reservations of their own choice, plus promises of goods and help in 'civilizing' their tribes.

Despite promises that the Indians could stay on their land until the various treaties were ratified by the Senate, Stevens at once allowed settlers into the treaty lands. Miners entered them, heading for strikes in British Columbia and northern Washington. The result was war,

54

though it was never a war in the true sense of the word, but a series of outbreaks. The Nez Percé, keeping to their treaty, refused to join in, as did Chief Seattle of the Duwamish League of Puget Sound. The Yakima were the heart of the rebellion, even attacking river steamers. After his defeat, the great Kamiakan managed to escape to Canada. General Crook, later to be a famous fighter against the Apache and the Sioux, vividly described conditions in this little-known war in his *Autobiography*:

It was no infrequent occurrence for an Indian to be shot down in cold blood, or a squaw raped by some brute. Such a thing as a white man being punished for outraging an Indian was unheard of ... The trouble with the army was that the Indians would confide in us as friends and we had to witness this unjust treatment of them without the power to help them. Then when they were pushed beyond endurance and would go on the war path we had to fight when our sympathies were with the Indians.

East of these unfortunate Indians were the Blackfoot Indians. The scourge of American mountain men, they were ready to trade with the British posts farther north. They were the only tribe to give real trouble to Lewis and Clark, and later American travelers suffered, too. Today, they live on both sides of the international border. Their worst experience of white hostility came in January 1870. The Piegan were the most southerly tribe of the Blackfoot Confederacy. Major Eugene M Baker, with two squadrons of the Second Cavalry, virtually destroyed a Piegan village on the Marias River, killing 120 men and 53 women and children. There had been Indian depredations before, but, not for the first time, soldiers attacked the wrong camp. There was so much uproar in the East over the massacre that a move to transfer the Indian Department to the War Department was quashed. The wretched tribesmen, ravaged also by smallpox, were in no mood to renew the conflict.

Across the border, despite growing food shortages caused by the decimation of the buffalo herds, things were better ordered. It is only fair to note that there was never a settler versus Indian problem in the Canadian West, even when the wars were at their fiercest below the border. Given that, the North-West Mounted Police—tough and just, though paternalistic—were trusted by Indians in a way no law enforcement body, military or civilian, ever was below the border. The Mounties had been formed in 1873, and, in 1874, 300 scarlet-coated men marched westward. American whiskey-traders vanished from their outpost at Fort Whoop-up in what is now Alberta, and a treaty was made with the Blackfoot Indians under their great Chief, Crowfoot. 'If the police had not come to this country, where would we all be now?' he was to say later. 'Bad men and whiskey were killing us so fast that few of us would be left today.'

The late 1870s saw campaigns in the North-west against other tribes, including the Bannock and 'renegade' Bannock, and the Shoshones known as Sheepeaters. The Bannock were joined by the Paiute in a war which, so General Crook later said, was caused by 'Hunger. Nothing but Hunger.' After long marches through rugged country and a number of battles, the Indians gave up the hopeless struggle.

Better known was the war against the Ute. Cattlemen and sheepherders like their Navaho enemies, they ranged widely in Utah and New Mexico. From the 1850s, they sided more often than not with the whites as auxiliaries. They had a good friend in Kit Carson, the ex-mountain man, and through him settled in western Colorado. There were some 3500 of them in six bands.

Ouray was their most influential chief. Bowing to the inevitable—there was a silver boom in the area, complete with a flood of miners—he ceded a quarter of the reservation. It was not enough for Coloradans, who wanted the Ute out altogether. They claimed that virtually every crime in Colorado was the work of the Ute. Ouray, who was seriously ill, could barely keep his people in check.

Fortunately for the Coloradans, they got a genuine atrocity to boost their desires in late 1879. At the White River Agency, there was an eccentric old agent, Nathan Meeker, who, among other ideas, had hoped to start a Uto-

LEFT: *Nathan Meeker, killed by the Utes of the White River Agency in 1879.* RIGHT: *Josephine Meeker, who was captured and outraged by the Utes in the uprising.*

pian colony. He also had a dream in which 'his' Ute would be instantly civilized and become self-sufficient farmers. Tact was not in him and his charges were becoming mutinous.

He now demanded troops, but no one seemed to think that the matter was urgent. On 10 September, Chief Douglas beat him up and his urgent request for help was answered. Major Thornburgh, with a cavalry troop and a company of infantry, set out from Fort Steele, Wyoming, picking up more troops as he went. He soon had 153 soldiers and 25 civilians.

The enraged Indians, believing that they would be sent in chains to Indian Territory, met Thornburgh some 60 miles from the agency and told of their feelings about Meeker. Their leader was a fierce young brave called Jack.

Meeker, now very alarmed, agreed with the Ute plan to have Thornburgh advance to the agency with only five men, there to parley with the chiefs. Although the major agreed, he finally decided that his troops should be stationed near the agency. Naturally, the Ute felt they were being betrayed.

Thornburgh left the infantry and eight wagons behind and, with 120 troopers, crossed into the reservation. They came upon Jack with 100 warriors and, after some talk and a shot fired, perhaps by an Indian, a battle began. Thornburgh was killed and a fight lasted several hours, the Ute almost managing to burn out the troops

by setting grass and sagebrush on fire. The new commander, Captain Payne, sent for help.

Fighting continued, and, on the 29th, the Ute killed Meeker and nine of his men and captured Mrs Meeker, her daughter Josephine and another woman and her two children. Mrs Meeker, Josephine and the other woman were raped.

The news of the battle brought troops by train and by road. Not until 5 October did the main relief force under Colonel Wesley Merrit arrive, and the Indians gave up the siege of Payne and his men. A few hours later, Merrit received a copy of a letter from Chief Ouray to the White River chiefs. In it, they were told to stop fighting as Jack and his band had agreed to do. Fearing the worst, Merrit marched to the White River agency and found the bodies.

News of the killings and the captives caused a national sensation. Troops were rapidly assembled and, finally, there were 1500 men in the field against the Ute. Despite bellicose statements from Generals Sherman and Sheridan, Carl Schurz, the wise and able Secretary of the Interior, decided that a major war would bring the rest of the Ute into action and result in the murder of the captives. He felt that Ouray's in-

fluence might prove decisive in getting the captives freed. Charles Adams, once a Ute agent, was asked to lead the peace mission and, despite military anger and fierce arguments among the Ute, he succeeded. It was a near thing, the tide being turned when Ouray's representative—the great Ute being ill—threatened on his leader's behalf to send the rest of the Ute nation against the White River hostiles.

The rebels were to go unpunished, it being decided that they had been forced to fight Thornburgh. However, an exception was made in the case of the 12 Indians judged to have been guilty of the killings and rapes at the agency. Yet it proved impossible to isolate the guilty Indians with the exception of Chief Douglas who was punished by being sent to Fort Leavenworth prison. His rape of Mrs Meeker was not mentioned publicly in order to avoid embarrassment to her.

The unfortunate Ute were punished by being driven into barren country in Utah. The only Ute, or, indeed, Indians, left in Colorado were the Southern Ute, who were given a narrow band of territory on the southwestern border of the state that had once been home to other great tribes, including the Comanche, Kiowa, Cheyenne and Arapaho. Ouray died in 1880, aged 47, just before the final dispersal of his people.

Chief Joseph was a great leader of the Nez Percé. The story of his people's downfall starts with his father, also Joseph, who got his name from Reverend Spalding. Old Joseph was born a Cayuse, but he married a Nez Percé and became a member of a tribe that had welcomed Lewis and Clark and every white man after them. No Nez Percé had ever killed a white, and, in return, many whites deeply admired the handsome and intelligent Nez Percé.

Old Joseph attended the 1855 Walla Walla council. The Nez Percé treaty gave his band

LEFT ABOVE: A photograph of Ouray, the chief of the Uncompahgre Ute Indians. LEFT: Another Indian chief, Seattle, of the Suquamish tribe. The Suquamish lived on Puget Sound in the state of Washington.

their old and beloved homeland in the Wallowa Valley, where Oregon, Idaho and Washington meet. Despite the appearance of miners who found gold, and the building of Lewiston, the coming of settlers, and the ill-treatment of individual Nez Percé, the Indians kept the peace during the wars of the late 1850s.

Another council was held in 1863, giving the Wallowa Valley to the government and paving the way for settlers to move in. Old Joseph refused to sign this treaty and rightly raged against other chiefs who had never lived in the valley, but signed it away along with other tribal land. He tore up a New Testament that had been given to him and placed poles around the edges of his beloved domain. Meanwhile, settlers started moving into the land of the 'nontreaty' Indians, as they were called.

In 1871, Joseph died and his son, Young Joseph, took his place. His Indian name was Hinmaton-Yalaktit—Thunder Rolling in the Mountains—and he was about 30 years old.

Almost at once, he and his people were being ordered out of their valley by officials, but Joseph refused to budge. He asked for President Grant to intervene and, in June 1873, the President ordered part of the valley to stay in Nez Percé hands.

Commissioners arrived in the valley to organize a new Indian agency, but found that the Nez Percé wanted neither churches nor schools. Joseph made a subtle point when asked why he did not want the churches. 'They will teach us to quarrel about God,' he said, having had his fill of headhunters of various religious groups seeking converts.

It was too good to last. In 1875, the government went back on its word. Already settlers had come into the valley, followed by gold miners, who stole the tribes' magnificent horses and their cattle. Leading nontreaty Indians—White Bird, Looking Glass, Toohoolhoolzote, Eagle from the Light and others—argued with each other and Joseph over whether to fight now or try and live in peace. They decided to attempt the latter, but it was obvious that a single incident by an Indian or a settler could shatter the peace.

Back in 1874, the one-armed Civil War veteran, General Oliver Otis Howard, had become the commander of the Department of the Pacific. Known as the 'Christian General,' he had served after the war as head of the Freedmen's Bureau of the War Department for ex-slaves, and as founder and principal of a university for blacks in Washington, D.C. He had made peace with Cochise in 1872. Now he found himself sympathizing with the Nez Percé, but, as things turned out, he was not sympathetic enough. Remembering the Battle of the Little Bighorn in 1876, he feared an uprising in the Northwest. When an Indian was murdered by a settler, he decided to act, well-meaningly but cruelly.

A two-day council was held, the bemused Christian general quite failing to comprehend the Indians' love of their land. Worse, he confused it with a cult which was rampant among many of the tribes of the Northwest, known as the 'Dreamer' cult and militantly antiwhite. So Howard reported to the Government that if Joseph and his band were not moved to Lapwai by persuasion, force must be used.

Joseph decided that he must submit, but at a meeting in May 1877, he was given only 30 days to move. He pleaded that his stock could not be rounded up that quickly and that the Snake River was very high. Howard, whatever his private feelings may have been, was publicly unmoved.

Joseph and his subchiefs had no choice. Cavalry from Fort Walla Walla had already taken over the Wallowa Valley, and the Indians now gathered up their stock, Joseph being well aware that there was not enough room for it at Lapwai. The tribe gathered at Hell's Canyon on the Snake, which was turbulent from the spring rains. Young Nez Percé on their finest horses towed their people across on rafts, not one being lost. However, the next day many mares and cows, colts and calves, were swept down the river. The Indians joined other Nez Percé, the Salmon River bands of Chiefs Toohoolhoolzote and White Bird, and settled on Camas Prairie below the reservation boundary to put off the move to Lapwai for the ten remaining days before the deadline expired.

Naturally, the braves were split on the subject of future action, or inaction, then, on 13 June, three youths, bolstered by whiskey, killed four white men who were notorious for their bad treatment of Indians. Joseph and his brother Ollokot tried to calm their people, saying that they would explain to Howard, but they had lost their hold on the younger warriors, 16 of whom rode off and killed 14 or 15 whites, then went on an orgy of drinking and looting.

There could be no turning back now. Chief Joseph later said that he would have given his own life if he could have undone the killing of the white men. He blamed his young men and the whites. 'I would have taken my people to the buffalo country Montana without fighting, if possible.'

So the heroic 1700-mile march began over some of the most rugged terrain in North America. At the end, 2000 troops were to be chasing the fugitives, not counting civilian volunteers and Indian scouts. 'Think we shall make short work of it,' Howard wired his superiors. Meanwhile, Joseph was ordering his chiefs to see that the young braves left white women and children unharmed.

On 16 June, the Nez Percé camped near the

Salmon River at White Bird Canyon. They hoped to collect stock, then head westward to avoid fighting, but that was not to be. They set a trap for the troops already pursuing them, and waited.

Between 60 and 70 warriors were ready for action, about the same number having drowned their sorrows in drink to such an extent that they were unfit for action. Against them rode Captain David Perry with just over 100 men of the First Cavalry, plus 11 civilians. Even at this late hour, the Indians made a final effort to effect a truce, but one of the men in the skirmish line commanded by Lieutenant Edward Theller fired twice despite a flag of truce. The Nez Percé war had begun.

The soldiers suffered a humiliating and heavy defeat. Theller and 33 of his men were killed, the Indians suffering just three wounded. After a brief hiatus, while the Indians decided what to do next and the whites fled to towns, Howard, with almost 400 men, marched from Fort Lapwai on 22 June 1877 to be joined by yet more troops, giving him over 400. On 1 July, Howard crossed the Salmon into mountainous country, and the Indians crossed back again. The troops could not manage the crossing and it took them five days to recross at the original spot used.

On 6 July, the bands of Chiefs Looking Glass and Red Echo appeared at Joseph's camp on the south fork of the Clearwater. This brought the Nez Percé force up to approximately 150 warriors, together with some 550 women, children and older men.

At this point it must be stressed that the fighting retreat was run by leading Indians in council, with Looking Glass the most notable of the leaders. Joseph, who at White Canyon appeared to have divided his time between fighting and getting the camp with its noncombatants on the

LEFT: *This illustration by Frederic Remington shows the surrender of Chief Joseph of the Nez Percé tribe of Indians to U.S. Army troops.* LEFT ABOVE: *Another version of that surrender.*

move, was the political and inspirational leader of the fugitives, as modern historians have made known. Whites never understood the fact that Indian leaders rarely had the degree of authority of white commanders, and it was naturally assumed that Joseph was indeed the military genius of the retreat. He had been dubbed the 'Red Napoleon', but until very near the end of the retreat he had no major influence on strategy. It suited white commanders, made to look so foolish by the Nez Percé, to claim that they were up against the genius of Joseph. In fact, they were facing collective genius. Joseph had the honored post of organizing the camp and the safety of the women and children.

For a short while, the fugitives rested. It was time to prepare for the march, mend equipment, and graze cattle and horses—more than 2000 animals in all. Suddenly, on 11 July, artillery fire opened up unexpectedly and a two-day battle began. It was fought with grim determination by both sides. Howard was to claim that 23 Indians had been killed, though they later stated that only 4 had died. He did admit that 'they fought as well as any troops I ever saw.' One of his officers stated flatly that the Nez Percé were not defeated and that their retreat was 'masterly, deliberate and unmolested, leaving us with a victory barren of results.'

At a meeting on 15 July, some of whose details are obscure, it seems that Looking Glass suggested trying to find a home with the Crows, and, if not, with Sitting Bull in Canada. The great Sioux leader had now joined the hundreds of Sioux who had fled there in the aftermath of Custer's Last Stand. Whatever happened, the Indians started climbing the Lolo Trail the next day, en route for the buffalo ranges. The journey was a cruel one, but in 11 days they reached Montana.

In the Bitterroot Valley, they came upon a road block manned by Captain Charles Rawn, 35 soldiers, some 200 volunteers, and a band of Flathead Indians. The chiefs politely asked if they might pass and Rawn understandably refused. However, his volunteers thought otherwise, believing the Nez Percé claim that settlers would be unharmed, and the Indians went through. They passed through the Bitterroot Valley, buying provisions at a store and paying

for goods that they found in an empty house. This was an Indian campaign the like of which none had experienced.

Looking Glass decided that the marchers needed a rest. This was a mistake, for Colonel Gibbon was near with 15 officers and 146 men, later to be joined by 45 volunteers. On 9 August, a dawn assault took the Nez Percé by surprise. It was a vicious attack in which women and children died, though women fought, too, alongside the men. Joseph and Looking Glass led a counterattack and Gibbon was forced to retire. The marksmanship of the Indians was noticeably better than that of the whites.

Now, with Joseph organizing the camp's retreat, a handful of warriors held off Gibbon's soldiers. Looking Glass was blamed for the decision to rest, while Nez Percé morale was shaken by the losses. And Howard was on the march again, only a day behind the Indians. He was halted by a sudden attack, then the fugitives crossed into Yellowstone Park (the first national park, created just five years before and now being enjoyed by its first visitors).

The Indians entered the park on 22 August 1877. There were still tourists in the area, two of whom were killed. Meanwhile, Looking Glass had gone ahead to sound out the Crows, hoping that they would succor the Nez Percé, but they had helped the army too often to wish to help its enemies. So the Nez Percé realized that Canada was their only hope. The Sioux had been their enemies, but surely things had changed and Sitting Bull, a refugee in Canada, would welcome them. Now, more than ever, Joseph was their inspiration.

One of several columns pursuing them was the late Colonel Custer's regiment, the Seventh Cavalry, suitably replenished after the debacle of the Little Big Horn 13 months before. The Nez Percé escaped from it after a skirmish. Howard, despairing of catching the Indians, sent an urgent message to the ambitious but efficient Colonel Nelson A Miles at Fort Keogh to march northward and cut the fugitives off.

The Nez Percé, slowed down by their sick and wounded, also pressed northward. It was fall. By the end of September, they were within 40 miles of the Canadian border. It was the time to rest a little and find some food. They did not know that Miles was near.

But his Cheyenne scouts had seen the fugitives at their Bear Paw encampment, and soon Miles was there with 600 men. A ferocious fight ensued, Miles later calling the enemy the best Indian marksmen he had ever seen. The whites lost more men than the Indians, though Toohoolhoolzote and Joseph's brother Ollokot died that day. It was another proof of the skill of the Nez Percé that their marksmen concentrated on officers and non-commissioned officers, killing seven sergeants of the Seventh. Two officers were also killed and four severely wounded.

Yet the Indians' position was now desperate. Five inches of snow had fallen, all their ponies were gone, and the only hope was that the messengers who had headed north to Sitting Bull's camp might bring him back with his braves to fight alongside them. Meanwhile, Joseph had to watch the misery of the children crying with hunger and cold, and old people suffering stoically in silence.

Miles decided to invite them to a parley. White Bird and Looking Glass refused to attend, but Joseph went. Nothing came of the talks except treachery, for Miles refused to let Joseph go. Fortunately, Lieutenant Jerome, under the impression that the Nez Percé were going to surrender, wandered into their positions and was taken prisoner, so Miles was forced to release Joseph as a trade for Jerome.

On 4 October, the fourth day of the siege, Howard arrived, much to the annoyance of Miles, who was outranked. However, he was informed that Howard would not assume command until the enemy had surrendered.

Looking Glass and White Bird still had hopes of getting help from Sitting Bull, and at a council on 5 October opposed Joseph, who wanted to reopen talks with Miles. It looked as if the Nez Percé would divide on the issue. Then, as the council ended, Looking Glass, by now determined to head northward, was hit in the forehead by a bullet that killed him instantly. That was that. 'I went to General Miles and gave myself up,' said Joseph later. Miles promised that the Indians could spend the winter at the military post on the Yellowstone, then return to Lapwai in the spring.

The story of the surrender has always belonged to Joseph because of his magnificent and heartbreaking speech, climaxed by the words: 'From where the sun now stands I will fight no more forever.' Sadly, Colonel Mark Brown, in *Montana*, January 1972, exposed the way in which Howard's aide-de-camp, Captain Charles Erskine Scott Wood, decided to improve on an already moving scene by inventing a surrender speech, when there is no actual proof that such a speech was made, or even that Joseph spoke any words at all. It is better therefore to quote what Wood wrote for the *Century Magazine* in 1884:

It was nearly sunset when Joseph came to deliver himself up. He rode from his little camp in the hollow. His hands were clasped over the pommel of his saddle, and his rifle lay across his knees; his head was bowed down. Pressing around him walked five of his warriors; their faces were upturned and earnest as they murmured to him; but he looked neither to the right nor the left, yet seemed to listen intently. So, the little group came slowly up the hill to where General Howard, with an aide-de-camp, and General Miles waited to receive the surrender. As he neared them, Joseph sat erect in the saddle, then gracefully and with dignity he swung himself down from his horse, and with an impulsive gesture threw his arm to its full length, and offered his rifle to General Howard. The latter motioned him toward General Miles, who received the token of submission.

Those present shook hands with Joseph, whose worn and anxious face lighted with a sad smile as silently he took each offered hand. Then, turning away, he walked to the tent provided for him.

Just over 400 surrendered with Joseph, less than a quarter being warriors. Ninety-eight warriors and some 200 women and children escaped across the Canadian border to Sitting Bull's camp in a pitiable condition, where they were welcomed by the Sioux and cared for. Later, some were to make the long trek home, only to find that they were regarded as troublemakers by those Nez Percé who had stayed behind.

Meanwhile, the aftermath of the poignant surrender was bitter indeed. Sherman wanted no part of Miles's promises. 'I believed Miles or I would never have surrendered,' Joseph was later to say. But, of course, those who had grabbed the Indians' lands did not want the Nez Percé back, even though, for once, the vast majority of Americans, including many Westerners, were on the Indians' side. When the captives passed through Bismarck, Dakota Territory, the townspeople cheered them, gave them food in the town square and laid on a special banquet for Joseph.

The captives were taken to Fort Leavenworth, Kansas, where more than 20 of them died of malaria that winter. After more moves in Kansas, and 47 more deaths, Joseph was allowed to visit Washington to plead for his peo-ple. They were sent to another reservation, this time in Indian Territory, where more of them died, including Joseph's baby daughter. By 1883, the scandalous treatment of the heroic Indians forced Congress to allow the Secretary of the Interior to act. So on 22 May 1885, 268 Nez Percé went back to the Northwest by train. Only 118 were allowed to go to the Lapwai reservation, the rest, including the 'dangerous' Chief Joseph, were sent to the Colville reservation in Washington.

Joseph was allowed back to his old home twice, in 1899 and in 1900. On the first visit, he tried to buy a plot of land and failed. On the second, it was made very clear to him that he would never succeed in getting what he so longed for. On 21 September 1904, he died of a broken heart, according to the agency doctor.

INDEX

ACKNOWLEDGMENTS

The author and publisher would like to thank the following people who have helped in the preparation of this book: Anistatia Vassilopoulos, who designed it; Thomas G Aylesworth, who edited it; Karin Knight, who prepared the index.

PICTURE CREDITS

All pictures were supplied by Peter Newark's **Western Americana.** In addition, the author would like to thank the following:
American Museum of Natural History: 52.
Library of Congress: 19 (top right), 42–43 (center).
Oklahoma State Senate: 24 (below).
Oliver Yates Collection: 14 (center), 23 (center), 38–39.
Simon Trent: 33 (left).
Smithsonian Institution, National Anthropological Archives: 14 (top right and bottom left), 32 (left), 37 (below), 47 (above).
State Capitol, Helena, Montana: 41 (top left).
Trustees of the British Museum: 25 (below).
United States National Park Service: 14 (top left), 43 (right), 44 (top), 45 (below), 47 (below).
Woolaroc Museum, Bartlesville, Oklahoma: 24 (above), 28–29, 45 (above).